SUMMARY

&ANALYSIS

OF

OUTER
ORDER

INNER
CALM

DECLUTTER & ORGANIZE
TO MAKE MORE ROOM FOR HAPPINESS

A GUIDE TO THE BOOK
BY GRETCHEN RUBIN

NOTE: This book is a summary and analysis and is meant as a companion to, not a replacement for, the original book.

Please follow this link to purchase a copy of the original book: https://amzn.to/2FclrlO

TABLE OF CONTENTS

SYNOPSIS

Gretchen Rubin's *Outer Order, Inner Calm: Declutter & Organize to Make More Room for Happiness* is a practical book that explains how you can live a happier life by simply cleaning up the messes around you. Living and working in a disorderly environment creates a feeling of restlessness which can sap your energy over time. Rubin believes that achieving a balanced and calm life is possible by managing your possessions better.

The book is divided into five chapters laid out in a specific sequence of steps. The first step in achieving outer order and inner calm is making choices. Rubin explains why clutter is such a major challenge for most people and how anyone can figure out what to keep and what to get rid of. After that, you must take action and create the order you want to see in your life.

In the third chapter, she talks about the importance of knowing yourself and others. Just because you are bothered by clutter doesn't mean others feel the same way. She offers advice on how to declutter while maintaining harmony. The fourth step involves cultivating the right habits so that once you have cleaned out your clutter, it doesn't sneak back in. Finally, she recommends that you add beauty to your now decluttered space. You can go the extra step of making the room come alive by incorporating colors, scents, and sounds to refresh your room.

Ultimately, the whole point is to fulfill your inner calm. If decluttering makes you happy, do it because it is worth the effort. You should always be in control of your possessions, not the other way around.

CHAPTER ONE: MAKE CHOICES

Rubin opens the book by explaining why clearing clutter is such a huge challenge for most people. She states that the biggest hurdle is in deciding which of your possessions to keep and which ones to throw out. The first step is to ask yourself *why* you possess all that stuff in the first place. There are many excuses that you can give for having cluttered surroundings. But you must be prepared to make some tough choices. However, it is important to note that creating outer order is more about wanting what you have rather than living with fewer possessions.

Key Takeaway: To make the decluttering process easier, you must be well-prepared.

The decision-making process tends to sap people's energy, which is why deciding what to clear out can be so difficult. Rubin suggests that you prepare yourself by getting enough sleep, eating a healthy meal, and probably drinking some caffeine. If possible, ask someone to help you when decluttering your space. You should also have enough tools and equipment at hand. Part of your preparation involves knowing how to treat a particular possession—should it stay or should it go? There are three questions you need to ask: *"Do I need this?" "Do I love this?" and "Do I use this?"* It's okay to have an item that meets at least one of these criteria. However, if you possess an item that you don't need, love, or use, then it should definitely be thrown out or given away.

Key Takeaway: Identify who can benefit from your clutter and give stuff away quickly.

According to Rubin, it is easier to get rid of items when you have already identified people who are likely to benefit from them. Find individuals or organizations that can benefit from old toys, books, clothes, food packs, board games, unused drug prescriptions, furniture, etc. However, you have to be careful not to allow the stuff you are giving away to accumulate in your home or office. The moment you identify your beneficiaries, pack and send off the items. You do not want a bunch of boxes of unused items staying in a corner for months, creating more clutter.

Key Takeaway: Embrace technology to help clear clutter.

There are times when you hold onto an item whose use has been replaced by technology. For example, there's no need to have user manuals lying around when you can easily look up the information online. You don't need that fax machine, CDs, maps, thesaurus, or calculator that you never use. Don't hang on to an outdated version of something if there is a new version that probably occupies less space. Another way to motivate yourself to declutter is to take a photo of an area. Looking at the photo will allow you to evaluate that particular area with a fresh perspective. This will help you identify which items to get rid of. On top of that, you can convince others of the need to clear the clutter by showing them the photo. Once you have cleared the clutter, take another photo as visual proof of your accomplishment.

Key Takeaway: Use a checklist to clear out your clothes closet.

As you examine every item of clothing you own, create a checklist of questions. Does the item fit you? Do you usually wear it? Is it in good shape? Is it comfortable? Is it out of fashion? Have you worn it fewer than five times? When was the last time you wore it? Does it match your other clothes? Do you need to fix it before you can wear it? Rubin says that you may not have to throw the item out. You can demote it and wear it around the house instead of out to dinner. If it has sentimental value or is only worn for costume parties, then remove it from your closet and place it elsewhere.

Key Takeaway: Watch out for the Endowment and Duration effect.

Clutter often results from accumulating free items or falling for supposed deals and bargains. Therefore, before you decide to take something home with you because of its low price, ask yourself whether you really need it, love it, or will ever use it. Once the item enters your house, you will find it very difficult to get rid of. Rubin refers to this as the "endowment effect," where you feel attached to an item simply because you possess it. On top of that, there is also the "duration effect," which is what happens when you possess an item for so long that it becomes more precious over time. The longer you keep an unused item, the harder it is to let go of, so make up your mind and get rid of it as quickly as possible.

Key Takeaway: Paper and deep clutter are the worst forms of clutter.

According to Rubin, paperwork is hardest to get rid of because there is minimal satisfaction in tossing out old papers. Getting rid of paperwork also induces anxiety because your mind tells you that you may be throwing out some vital document. She recommends that you determine whether the piece of paper is of use, is outdated, can be replaced or scanned, or can be accessed online. Deep clutter is those invisible items that have been stored away nicely yet you don't use, need, or love. Good examples are business cards and notebooks.

CHAPTER TWO: CREATE ORDER

After you make the decision on what to get rid of, the next step is to establish order in the previously cluttered areas. You have to learn how to organize and place everything where it belongs. According to Rubin, this step is difficult yet immensely satisfying and energizing. She provides tips on how to creating order and maintain a greater sense of control over all areas of your life.

Key Takeaway: If you tolerate small clutter, you are setting yourself up for a major mess.

The broken theory states that if you allow petty crime to continue, you will soon have to deal with more serious crimes. Rubin believes that the same holds true when it comes to clutter. If you allow a little disorder in your home or office, you will soon have to clear out large piles of clutter. Examples of broken windows include piles of trash, putting shoes in the wrong places, unsorted mail, and a messy bed. If you are not careful, certain areas in your house can quickly turn into clutter magnets. For example, if you develop the habit of dumping your clothes on the floor instead of the closet, you will begin to see all kinds of clutter accumulating on the floor. Clutter attracts clutter, so ensure that you get rid of any mounds before they turn into mountains.

Key Takeaway: The older you get the harder it is to clear clutter.

Decluttering your house is overwhelming, but for older people, it becomes nearly impossible. This is because older people have less energy, time and emotional strength to get rid of the possessions that they have become attached to. Research shows that people who are over 50 years of age are highly unlikely to get rid of or give away their possessions. This capacity actually reduces with every passing decade. Therefore, if you want to get rid of clutter, start as soon as possible. The longer you wait, the harder the process becomes.

Key Takeaway: In your active areas, identify the problems and keep the surface neat.

If you want to maintain order in your active workspaces, you should first identify specific problems and then sort them out. For example, if your sweater is somehow finding its way to your desk, get a hook or coatrack. If you are always losing pieces of paper with vital information, get a notebook or file folder for organizing your papers. Rubin suggests that you keep all your work surfaces bare instead of cramming all kinds of items and devices onto your active areas.

Key Takeaway: Walk through your house as a stranger and evaluate everything.

Rubin suggests that you should pretend to be a stranger or tourist and take a tour through your home or office. Look inside every closet, drawer, and cabinet and simply see what kind of items you have stashed away. This will enable you to see those areas where you have forgotten clutter that has accumulated over the years. You can also pretend to be a real estate agent and try to determine which aspects are lowering the value of the house. The reason why this works is that a stranger doesn't have any emotional connection to the possessions. This kind of detachment will make it easier to create order in your home or office.

Key Takeaway: Avoid the tendency to add clutter when eliminating clutter.

When it's time to declutter, some people instinctively rush to the store to buy storage containers. They assume that these containers will help them keep everything organized. Rubin states that such people actually generate the worst clutter because they make the process more complicated. Buying fancy storage containers is simply an expensive way to move clutter from one area to another. It's better to get rid of unnecessary items instead of stashing them in a place where they will soon be forgotten.

Key Takeaway: Don't confuse temporary and permanent situations.

If you want to create permanent order, you must ensure that you start off on the right foot from day one. For example, when you move into a new home, do not allow people to dump stuff wherever they wish. You may convince yourself that the disorder is temporary, but clutter may soon become a permanent aspect of your house. On the other hand, an item that appears to be a permanent feature in your house may turn out to be temporary. For example, that kitchen chair may not be around for long. Learn to focus on things that will become permanent.

Key Takeaway: Avoid friction by allocating separate holding bins.

If you are sharing a space with colleagues, family members, or roommates, then you don't want to create unnecessary friction when decluttering. Individuals see clutter different, and what may aggravate you may be fine for someone else. Therefore, to create order, place some holding bins in a convenient yet inconspicuous place. If people dump their stuff in the wrong place, just drop their possessions into a holding bin. This will save you the time you would have spent trying to figure out where to place their possessions. Make sure the bins are not located in common areas but are easily accessible by the owner of the items.

CHAPTER THREE:
KNOW YOURSELF – AND OTHERS

No two individuals are alike. As such, Rubin argues that there is no best way to clear clutter. One person may decide to get rid of stuff they don't need because material possessions are meaningless to them. Another person may choose to throw out only those things that they don't consider precious while keeping a few meaningful items. The underlying factor is to know yourself instead of trying to follow another person's methods. This also applies when sharing a space with other people. You have to know what they like or dislike when it comes to clutter. They may be okay with some types of clutter but not others. Understanding this will help create a more harmonious atmosphere.

Key Takeaway: Identify the reason for clearing your clutter.

Clearing clutter shouldn't be a mechanical process where you take on a task that doesn't have any meaning behind it. Rubin states that you need to know why you are doing it so that you end up utilizing your time and energy productively. Understanding the purpose behind it will prevent you from stopping halfway through a cleaning project. But once you have defined your purpose clearly, you will move with speed and feel more satisfied at the end of it all. On top of that, first deal with the kind of clutter that pisses you off the most instead of trying to clear everything at once.

Key Takeaway: Don't let a fantasy or outdated identity create clutter.

It is possible that you may be holding onto possessions that pander to some fantasy existence that you wish you were living. Some of these items may be a way for you to project a certain image to others so that you appear to be something you are not. Maybe you used to enjoy a certain lifestyle long ago but you refuse to get rid of items that you no longer use. For example, you used to ski but you hurt your knee. Despite the fact that you will never ski again, you still keep tons of skiing equipment lying around. Rubin suggests that you choose a few mementos and get rid of everything else.

Key Takeaway: You can either look at your possessions practically or mystically.

According to Rubin, a practical perspective is where you view all your items as inanimate objects. With a mystical view, you tend to see your possessions as spiritual items. For example, you cycle through all your plates so that none of them feels ignored. People with a mystical view tend to find it more difficult to get rid of clutter. However, Rubin recommends that you simply thank your old items for their years of service and then let them transition to the next stage of their life.

Key Takeaway: Sometimes you just have to mind your own business.

There is no reason for you to be bothered by clutter that belongs to someone else. If it isn't affecting you in any way, say, their desk is disorganized, just ignore it. There is no need to waste energy worrying about something that the person concerned doesn't perceive to be a problem.

Key Takeaway: Don't give gifts that people don't need.

Though gift-giving is a great tradition, make sure that you give someone an item that they really want. Rubin states that you should keep a wish list for yourself and others so that both you and your loved ones receive gifts that you actually want.

Key Takeaway: Figure out whether you are a sprinter or marathoner.

When clearing clutter, a sprinter expends a lot of effort within a short period of time to clean up an area. Such people thrive under pressure and deadlines, and they may invite friends over just to force themselves to clean up. Marathoners, on the other hand, tend to work slowly and steadily over time, choosing to clear clutter for a few minutes each day. They hate pressure and deadlines. According to Rubin, neither of these systems is better than the other, so choose the one that works best for you.

Key Takeaway: Your response to expectations will determine how best to clear your clutter.

Rubin believes that your personality framework can help you know how to optimize the process of clearing your clutter. She categorizes people into four groups:

Upholders – People who respond readily to all expectations and love to-do lists and schedules. Therefore, fit your cleaning tasks into your calendar.

Questioners – People who prefer to know why they are doing something before they do it. Therefore, find reasons to justify the importance of clearing your clutter.

Obligers – People who easily meet outer expectations. Therefore, ask someone to come over to keep you accountable as you clean.

Rebels - People who hate all expectations. Therefore, remind yourself that clearing clutter isn't about what others want. See it as a challenge to overcome.

Key Takeaway: Ask others for help instead of complaining.

It's easy to be passive-aggressive when cleaning other people's clutter. Rubin suggests that you ask people to help you instead of nagging them to clean up. This will help you prevent resentment from building up.

CHAPTER FOUR: CULTIVATE HELPFUL HABITS

Rubin claims that once you have made the right choices, created order, and understood yourself and others, the next step is to develop the right habits. These habits need to be easy and performed on a regular basis so that clutter doesn't pile up. You are better off managing your possessions every moment rather than trying to play catch up later on. This may feel tiresome at first, but once clutter management becomes an ingrained habit, the behavior becomes automatic.

Key Takeaway: Apply the one-minute rule to make your life easier.

Rubin explains the one-minute rule as the habit of performing any task that can be done in under a minute without delay. It takes less than one minute to hang your coat on a hanger, so do it instead of tossing it on the couch. It takes less than a minute to throw away a pen that has run out of ink, so do it immediately instead of returning it to the desk drawer. Such tasks can be accomplished quickly and easily to maintain a clutter-free environment.

Key Takeaway: Don't use clutter as an excuse to procrastinate important tasks.

Rubin explains how she sometimes avoids doing a meaningful yet unpleasant task by clearing her clutter. She convinces herself that she cannot do an assignment until her office shelves are clear, yet the truth is that she is simply procrastinating. Rubin refers to this phenomenon as "procrasticlearing." Though it's true that orderly office space is a great way to help you focus on work, you should never allow clutter-clearing to take precedence over important tasks. Ask yourself this question: "If I completed my important assignment, would I still want to clear the clutter?" If the answer is no, then you are procrasticlearing.

Key Takeaway: Create your own clutter-free space.

If you happen to be sharing a house with someone else, you should find a room that you can make your own. This room should be clutter-free so that if your housemate is messy, at least you can take refuge in your own clean area. However, if it isn't possible to have a room all to yourself, you can still find space for your personal items in a closet, drawer, cabinet, or file. Rubin states that you should guard your clutter-free space jealously. Do not allow anyone to place their items in your space. If it's not yours, it should never be found in your space.

Key Takeaway: If you can't sleep, get up and clean.

One of the recommendations that sleep experts give is to get out of bed and engage in a quiet activity if you cannot sleep. Rubin states that when she suffers from sleep trouble, she clears some clutter. This doesn't have to be too taxing or contemplative. She simply walks around her house and puts stuff in their rightful place. After about twenty minutes, she goes back to sleep. Even if you wake up the next day feeling a tad tired, at least your house looks neat.

Key Takeaway: Become a smart shopper to avoid buying needless items.

One of the reasons why you may be having so much clutter in your house is poor shopping habits. Rubin suggests that you never enter a store unless you need a specific item. Never stay in the store for too long and do not grab a basket because you may end up spending money on more stuff. You should also avoid trying free samples lest you are tempted to buy something you don't need, even if it seems like a bargain.

Key Takeaway: Save all your unpleasant tasks for "power hour."

Everyone has a bunch of tasks that they do not enjoy doing. If these tasks are not urgent, you are even more likely to postpone them. According to Rubin, this kind of procrastination will drain you of energy. The solution is to create a list of these tasks and work on them for one hour every week.

Key Takeaway: Always make your bed

Though this may seem like a simple and insignificant habit, Rubin claims that the majority of people say that making their bed makes them happier. The reason is that making your bed can be done very quickly and the end result is a well-ordered room. Your bedroom is a representation of you, so if it looks nice, you just feel better.

Key Takeaway: Avoid stockpiling stuff that you don't even use.

There's a limit to the number of rubber bands, shopping bags, baseball caps, and ketchup packets that you can reasonably use at any given time. So why accumulate such stuff in large quantities in the first place? Rubin recommends that you avoid acquiring such things, and if they are offered to you for free, just refuse to take them. Make sure that all your possessions have a purpose behind them.

Key Takeaway: Spend ten minutes every day transitioning from one task to the next.

Your daily life can be split into stages, with each stage being defined by a particular task. Rubin recommends that you take 10 minutes between stages to clear up any clutter. For example, before you leave the office at the end of the day, take 10 minutes to place every item in its rightful place. You should toss the trash in the bin, check your calendar for next day's tasks, close any open drawers, and pack up any item that belongs at home. If you are at home, spend 10 minutes in the evening putting everything in order. Shoes, coats, and chairs should be placed where appropriate and the kitchen counter wiped clean. Rubin refers to this habit as the "ten-minute closer."

CHAPTER FIVE: ADD BEAUTY

Rubin devotes this chapter to the concept of creating a beautiful environment. Outer order and inner calm must go beyond eliminating clutter. Once you have adopted regular habits to prevent clutter from accumulating, you must create a sense of beauty in your surroundings. This can be achieved through color, lighting, scent, and space. Adopting the right techniques will renew you and give you the opportunity to enjoy the inner calm that can only flow from outer order.

Key Takeaway: Select a color or pattern that defines your home.

There are many shades of colors that you can choose from to define your home. Choosing a signature color is a great way to add beauty and harmony to your surroundings, not to mention making it easier to decide which color to use for your personal items. Rubin also believes that a dash of color is enough to elevate your spirits. If you aren't keen on colors, maybe you should consider having a signature pattern, for example, animal print or denim material.

Key Takeaway: Create a child-free area in your home.

In case you live in a large house with your children, it may be a good idea to have a child-free zone where no kids are allowed to enter. Kids tend to create messes everywhere they go, so you need to have a separate space where you can enjoy order, privacy, and quiet. This can be your bedroom, lounge, or even just a corner of the house.

Key Takeaway: Create more space at work.

According to Rubin, a lot of people work in offices that feel cramped. Instead of simply dreaming about a larger workspace, you can make your existing work area more spacious and inviting. The first step is to remove any unnecessary items from your desk and drawers. If you don't use, need, or love it, get rid of it. Then ask some of your colleagues whether they would like to follow suit. By eliminating clutter from desks, hallways, and notice boards, the entire office will appear more spacious.

Key Takeaway: Establish a secret location for your household.

One way to add more life and satisfaction to your house is by creating a secret place where only close family members have access to. This could be an unseen closet, locked chest, or hidden drawer. You can find such a place when you are clearing clutter.

Key Takeaway: Maintain order even on your smartphone.

Your smartphone may have a lot of visual and audio clutter, such as unused apps, folders, and even notification sounds. Rubin suggests that you delete unused apps or move them from the first screen to other screens. You can also collect related apps and put them in one folder to create more space on your phone. If you want to prevent your phone from intruding into your life, turn off all sounds and get rid of needless notifications.

Key Takeaway: Bring nature and fragrance into your home.

Mother Nature has created her own sense of order. You can take this outdoor order and bring it into your home. Gather some pebbles, shells, pinecones, fern fronds, and flowers and create a beautiful arrangement indoors. You can also use scents to add fragrance to a room by lighting scented candles. The flickering flames can make a room come alive.

Key Takeaway: Eliminate visual noise

Visual noise can be created when you accumulate all kinds of stuff on one surface. For example, your fridge door may contain an assortment of magnets, old flyers, expired coupons, kid's artwork, and tattered clippings. This can make the kitchen look like a mess, even if the other surfaces in the room are well-arranged.

Key Takeaway: Beautify the entrance to your house.

One of the reasons why the entrance to the house becomes messy is that everyone wants to dump their stuff there the moment they step into the house. Shoes, bags, and coats can easily pile up at the entrance and quickly become an eyesore. Rubin suggests you place hooks, shelves, and baskets at the entrance and beautify the area using a mural, plant, or piece of art. It is important to feel a sense of calm the moment you step over the threshold of your home.

Key Takeaway: Create a luxurious feel in your space.

Adding beauty may mean spending a little bit extra on specific luxury items. Rubin states that you shouldn't be afraid to buy some Egyptian cotton sheets, a nice wallet, or a wonderful chef's knife. Such luxury items are functional and can make your life more pleasant. To add enjoyment to her work, Rubin says that she bought some brightly patterned files and a stylish book weight.

Key Takeaway: Always stay grateful for what you have.

Rubin believes that an attitude of gratitude is something that will make your life much happier. Sometimes the things you own can make you go crazy, but you should still be grateful for the fact that they serve you well. Your possessions are signs that you are loved and blessed.

EDITORIAL REVIEW

Outer Order, Inner Calm is Gretchen Rubin's latest book on how to declutter your life. Her goal is to teach us how to achieve greater happiness by creating more organized and orderly surroundings. Though some people would argue that living or working in a messy environment is a trivial issue, Rubin believes that being surrounded by all kinds of clutter creates the sense that you don't have much control over your life. The simple (though not always easy) act of clearing clutter can help you feel more energized physically, emotionally, as well as intellectually.

In the book, Rubin lays out five stages that you go through to create order in your environment. The first stage is making the right choices regarding what possessions to keep or get rid of. The second step is organizing your cluttered areas. The third stage involves gaining a better understanding of who you are and want you want to achieve from the decluttering process. At the same time, you have to know the people around you in terms of whether they are messy or neat. Once you have that figured out, you need to create habits that prevent the clutter from making a comeback. Finally, you should try to maintain a beautiful environment that brings comfort to you and others.

But why is it so necessary to live an ordered life? Well, according to Rubin, maintaining outer order is guaranteed to achieve nine things:

- Save time, energy, money, space, and patience

- Create more harmonious relationships

- Your home becomes a sanctuary

- Less guilt over wastage of possessions

- You feel more self-assured and positive

- You won't have to deal with people's judgment

- It highlights your current state of mind

- It creates a sense of renewal

- It creates a sense of purposefulness

The book is pretty short and to the point. Each of the five chapters contains short yet practical tips that you can easily put into practice. Rubin doesn't go into much detail with her tips because most of it is very obvious, for example, when she says that soap and water remove most stains. Though there's really little that you would say is eye-opening, there are times when she does offer something intriguing. For example, she quotes a study that shows that people over fifty years of age find it very hard to let go of stuff due to sentimental reasons. Therefore, you need to get rid of your clutter before you get too old.

Her style, as in all of her other books, is pretty casual. There's very little academic research and most of her hacks are things she has experienced or adopted in her personal life. This creates a more authentic feel to her work and adds to her credibility as a practical rather than theoretical writer.

It would be remiss not to address the similarities here between the Marie Kondo method (author of the #1 bestselling book, *The Life-Changing Magic of Tidying Up*) including thanking your items before throwing them away and bringing natural scents in to freshen up a space. While Marie asks readers if items "spark joy," Gretchen asks if you "need it, use it, love it." Kondo's book has recently exploded with a popular reality series on Netflix, and it seems probable that Rubin is simply jumping on the decluttering bandwagon with a similar message for her fans. Of course, if you're a fan of Rubin's books, the similarities in their methods or the timing of this book's release likely won't bother you much, if at all.

Will everyone agree with her advice to clean up clutter quickly instead of letting it pile up? Some people simply love their possessions too much to let go. Ultimately, what you decide to do with your surroundings is up to you. Rubin believes that you should only clean up your surroundings if it makes your life better and happier. What may seem like disorder to one person may be perfectly fine to another. But at the end of the day, without doubt, outer order is the biggest contributor to inner calm.

BACKGROUND ON AUTHOR

Gretchen Rubin is a bestselling author and podcaster who excels at providing people with practical advice on how to live a happier and more fulfilled life. She has authored multiple New York Times bestselling titles, including *The Four Tendencies, Better than Before,* and *The Happiness Project.* Her books have been translated into 30 languages, with over three million copies being sold worldwide.

She was born on December 15, 1965, in Kansas City, Missouri. Gretchen Anne Craft went to The Pembroke Hill School and joined Yale University in 1984. She graduated from Yale in 1989 with a degree in English. She later attended Yale Law School where she earned her JD (Juris Doctor) degree in 1994. Rubin has also worked as a lecturer at Yale School of Management and Yale Law School. She went on to serve as a clerk of the U.S. Court of Appeals for the Second Circuit as well as the Supreme Court before deciding to pursue a career in writing.

Rubin's books are thought-provoking and incredibly insightful. Her in-depth understanding of human nature, habits, and happiness have garnered a huge following. Through her podcast, *Happier with Gretchen Rubin*, she enlightens her followers on how to cultivate the habits of happiness. She also has a website, *www.gretchenrubin.com*, where she talks about her personal pursuit of happiness.

Rubin lives with her husband, James, and their two daughters in New York City.

TITLES BY GRETCHN RUBIN

Outer Order, Inner Calm: Declutter & Organize to Make Room for Happiness (2019)

The Four Tendencies: The Indispensable Personality Profiles That Reveal How to Make Your Life Better (and Other People's Lives Better, Too) (2017)

Better Than Before: What I Learned About Making and Breaking Habits--to Sleep More, Quit Sugar, Procrastinate Less, and Generally Build a Happier Life (2015)

Happier at Home: Kiss More, Jump More, Abandon Self-Control, and My Other Experiments in Everyday Life (2012)

The Happiness Project: Or, Why I Spent a Year Trying to Sing in the Morning, Clean My Closets, Fight Right, Read Aristotle, and Generally Have More Fun (2009)

Profane Waste (2006)

Forty Ways to Look at JFK (2005)

Forty Ways to Look at Winston Churchill: A Brief Account of a Long Life (2003)

Power Money Fame Sex (2006)

End of Book Summary

If you enjoyed this ZIP Reads publication, we encourage you to purchase a copy of <u>the original book.</u>

We'd also love an honest review on Amazon.com!

Made in the USA
Monee, IL
02 August 2023

40377172R00020